Waiting for a Name

Waiting for a Name

ELIZABETH JAIKARAN

SHANTI ARTS PUBLISHING
BRUNSWICK, MAINE

Waiting for a Name

Published by Shanti Arts Publishing

Cover and interior graphics designed by
Khalidah Abubaker of Creative Differences

Interior design by Shanti Arts Designs

Shanti Arts LLC
193 Hillside Road
Brunswick, Maine 04011
shantiarts.com

Printed in the United States of America

ISBN: 978-1-956056-61-7 (softcover)

Library of Congress Control Number: 2022947420

In the name of God, the Most Gracious, the Most Merciful.

For Nash.
My every answered prayer.
My homecoming.
My very own poem.

Contents

After weeks and weeks of no rain . . .

Overjoyed, Bibi Zaheeda jumped up . . .

Stunned, Bibi Zaheeda did not even feel . . .

And just then the skies became dark . . .

Acknowledgements

I have so many people to thank for supporting me through the process of creating this collection of poetry. To begin with, I would like to thank the following publications, wherein these poems were first featured:

Aftab: "Brown"
Bruk Out Media: "Clap When the Plane Lands";
   "The Immigrant Parent"; and "Is"
Human/Kind: "Antyesti"
Sorjo: "Sentinel Gifts"
South Asian American Digital Archive: "One Last Bag"
PREE: Wild Thing

I also want to thank, from the bottom of my heart, the supremely talented Rajiv Mohabir for his ongoing support and mentorship on this path of sharing my poetry with the world. Your friendship is such a boon and I don't ever take it for granted.

To the readers who have formed a beautiful community around my work, I thank you for lifting up my writing in ways I never thought imaginable.

Finally, I would like to thank my family and friends for being my steadfast pillars of support in times of heightened uncertainty. None of this is possible without you all.

Introduction

When I was eleven years old, my mother discovered a slim, spiral-bound, Winnie-the-Pooh notebook on my desk filled with poetry I had written over the course of two years. Likely believing it was an old subject notebook or a homework logger, she was surprised to find each page embossed with poetry, with the deliberate indentations of a writer pressing too hard on her pen. My mother read all of the poems in a single night, and later that week, one evening after dinner, she called me into her bedroom.

"I found your poems," she said, smiling warmly, the bright yellow journal in her hands. "I want to send these to a publisher!" I was so focused on the fact that she had discovered my poems that I didn't even process her suggestion to share them further than the perimeter of our Queens home. She hugged me, told me she was so proud, and a bunch of other things that my ears were too hot to hear. I retrieved my notebook from her hands and went back to my room, where I quietly ripped the pages to shreds.

I doused baby oil on the destroyed pieces of my young, poetic prowess that lay defeated in the trash so that if anyone touched them, the ink would smear on the glossy paper. They could never be repaired. I was so completely ashamed to have had my poetry read by eyes other than my own—poems I wasn't sure were "good," about feelings I wasn't sure how to articulate.

I still remember some of those pages. The wide-ruled blue lines filled with large, loopy letters, all in black ink. Even as a child, I knew the importance of having a single writing pen to make the process a bit more comfortable for myself. I remember the long stanzas and refrains of rhyming couplets. The proclamations of feeling "broken" and later "healed."

I have been writing prose since I was eight years old, but poetry was different for me back then. Those poems tracked the period of my earliest adolescent emotional development, and I destroyed them all because I was embarrassed and ashamed of my own creative mind. I was positive that I was not a real poet. I was just a kid with a notebook and certainly not good enough for readership outside of myself. "No one will ever read these again," I vowed.

It was a full year before I wrote another poem. My seventh-grade homeroom teacher pushed me very early in the semester to join an after-school spoken word program, without knowing very much about me or how it would change my life. After some reluctance, I agreed to enroll. That program revitalized me in a way that infantilized any imposter syndrome I had as a writer. Taught by people of color, with a class comprised almost entirely of students of color from all over New York City, 4:30 pm on Tuesdays became my favorite time of the week. We would work on various poetry writing prompts and then share our work with the most supportive group of classmates anyone has ever known. I wish every New York City public school student could experience it. After just a week in the spoken word program, I began writing poetry in earnest again and even became inspired to take other genres more seriously.

I started writing stories. I started a blog for classroom news called LIZZIE'S NEWS—oh, what vain titling! But it showed just how much my confidence had replenished itself since the destruction by baby oil just one year prior. I fell, once again, so deeply in love with writing and felt secure enough to share my work without fear. I posted poems to my "away" messages on instant messenger. I distributed printouts of my news articles to classmates. I was a full out writer, if anyone asked me.

After high school, poetry was eventually de-prioritized by my desire to develop as a prose writer. I took workshop after workshop, even enrolling in a writing course in London, all under the banner of this pursuit. And then one day, it just happened again. I jotted down in my journal a brief string of thoughts that manifested during a free-writing session. When I put down my pen and looked back at those words, I was surprised to find a poem staring back at me. In that moment, I was shocked to see how much she had changed.

We picked up right where we left off. After writing my first book and later embracing my new life as a practicing attorney, I've found that poetry has been the kind of friend I can count on even with limited time to engage with creative expression. On the train going home, on lunch breaks, or right before bed, it is there to help me digest and process my everyday happenings and thoughts, either through my own writing or through my exposure to the bottomless pool of poetry available for digital consumption. A completely undemanding, yet still consuming and fulfilling, friendship. Even when I feel depleted, without much to offer the world, poetry allows me under her shade and steadily fills my cup.

When I decided to compile my poetry for this book, I was delighted to find diversity in my own written form over the years. In one year, I was extremely devoted to long-form lamentations. In another year, bite-sized ruminations were my affinity. Most recently, free verse has become my goal. While it is true that poets have their distinct styles, it is also true that we are perpetually growing, like anyone or anything else, and that our styles change accordingly. It is also true that we possess a number of styles within us—each one in our literary arsenal to be used for a particular emotion or message we wish to convey. I believe this collection to be a reflection of this poetic versatility.

I feel so lucky to have discovered poetry so early in life, such that I have been able to meaningfully engage with difficult topics during my formative years (like the complicated recurring themes of diaspora and homeland in the myriad poetic forms contained in this book). Of all writing forms, poetry is the dearest to me, for what it allows me to create and the magic it allows me to witness from others.

If I could go back, I would stop myself from destroying the poetry of my young mind. I would give so much just to have a glimpse of what I was feeling and thinking, and how I chose to express those feelings as a young writer. I probably would have included some of those poems in this work. But even that reactionary childhood destruction and fear was part of the great love story that poetry and I share. What once was shame has become devotion, and I no longer know where the poetry ends and I begin.

There once was a woman named Bibi Zaheeda, who lived in a small house the color of persimmon on the west coast of the Big River.

Each morning she began her day by brushing her teeth on the second-floor verandah and spitting the frothy paste and filmy water onto the rusty zinc roof below, with splashes that resembled the way she loved—in small, excited explosions. Then she would thump her way down the stairs to retrieve rainwater from the blue plastic barrel that had once held garments and sweets and canned goods from a place where excess grows like fuzzy moss.

Each time Bibi Zaheeda washed her face with the Blue Barrel Rainwater, her skin shed its blemishes and her features arranged themselves into a formation most people found stunning, and light as pure as an Eid moon glowed through her pores onto anyone who looked her way. It was a secret she kept from all, preferring them to believe her countenance to be natural-born and lucky.

One day the Blue Barrel Rainwater was done, down to the last droplet of condensation, and rainfall was not expected for weeks. So Bibi Zaheeda confined herself to her house the color of persimmon, refusing to leave while not armed with the secret elixir of her beauty.

Brown

brown like Demerara sugar.
the kind of tone that glows yellow in the dead winter months.
almost fluorescent.
cadaverous.
kin to the spirits of those upon whose legacies
we stand.
straighten your back.

Kohinoor

there are curious
sproutings in these
west indies.
hiding between the blades
of grass. a rich camouflage
that is both
natural
and unbelonging.
a treasure stolen
piece by piece.
limb by limb.
contract by contract.
gems fit for the
mother's crown.
a people rubbed with
adversity,
until they
shone, polished.
cold.

Woman of Color

some days I want to be
conciliatory and gentle,
a diplomat in the barter for my humanity.
and some days I want to be
maa kali,
adorned with the skulls of
my oppressors around my neck.

Inheritance

"wow, what a temper."
sometimes I do not know
if I am a woman or if
I am a storm.

or perhaps all of the women
before me, whose mouths
were wired shut by tradition,
incapable of expressing their
rage.
perhaps now they scream,
wildly,
through me.

Sentinel Gifts

Life has taken so much from
Granny. But it left behind all of her
fears.
A cabinet left unopened and unraided.
For that it has no use.
Her joys, her opinions, her memories—
she laid them down,
surrendered them. And they were collected
and packed away someplace so far away
that she doesn't know how to get there,
all while her amygdala tends
a neat graveyard of
her worst days and switch blades
hidden in sleeves,
right atop her lap.

> Each day I reintroduce myself.
> She smiles when a flicker of memory
> flashes across
> the hippocampus where two decades of
> my rearing
> spike to nothingness like mold.
> I tell her I am a professional.
> I tell her I am a mother.
> I tell her I am happy.
> There is no response.

I tell her I am married and her
lips labor to move and twist. Her tongue careens
over canyons
    of teeth and no teeth.

            "Have an account that only you know about," she says.
A spirit suddenly exorcised
she
collapses smaller in her seat, exhausted from having made
    the effort to parse through bodies and
rob their graves to
bring me this weapon she will not set down for
as long as she must tend remains in her lap.

Antyesti

everyone wondered why his
ashes
floated atop the water like that.
his children had to drown him
in death
hands and fists on buoyant powdery bone
to announce a final resting
in gingery waves slurping shores
embossed with a collar of boot prints.

sunlight breaking in refraction
ash refracting to atoms
in downward fight
reaching for air
and dervishing to the floor the same.

these waters are a grieving
his children thought
ash refracting to atoms snowing
on a lukanani's back.
only sweet water burial for dem daddy.

They Gave Us Gifts

children of indenture.
        our ancestors gave us so much more
than trauma and scars
scabbed by history.

they also gave us roots to be unshakable.

they gave us wings to be limitless.

Clap When the Plane Lands

At 33,000 feet the line
for the bathroom abandons
piety to the glowing seatbelt signs and
the pilot hisses warning of turbulence,
                    but who knew clouds could be so bumpy?

Dis side and dah side the
aircraft clambers as though
lobster walking through a crowd
at Saturday Market.
The tail jumps and falls while
crinkling aluminum foil chorus,
celestial harps revealing
aloo ball et al.,
much better than airline sandwiches, how wise.

The serenity of it all. Fried dough
dipping into and out of sour the color of pus, and
of dry sacred butter, depending on who you are.
On an open tray, a depressed empty hole,
waiting for the lady to bring back a cokes.

Who can ever run this fast
four hundred miles per hour
away from home,
                    toward home.

The journey feeling nothing more
than a lazy nap with anesthetized ears
in a pressurized cabin.

Wheels pound on tarmac
a foot stomping
like a devadasi in aramandi.
What a performance.

Reframing

For some reason.
I could never shake it out of my head.
When I learned that my father's *madrassa*
taught him Urdu. And not
the sacred Arabic of al-Qur'an.
There in that pocket of
rice and
sugar and
strangeness turned life.
That *aliph, be, pe* was decidedly necessary over *alif, ba', ta'*.
That the tongue of Mirza mattered more than the
tongue of revelation.
Perhaps it is the clear directive of it all.
That reuniting with your mother tongue
is an act of worship.
That paradise.
Will look
just like home.

Du'as in Shalwars

when my people pray
they also drape themselves
in the clothing of the old country.
such is our ancestral history.
a sacred ritual.
a prayer.
a beloved
distant
God.

I think I hated myself before I left
the safe encasement of the walls of my
mother. I think I hated the way my skin
absorbed light before I could even gaze
upon the skin of another.
I think I heard the voices before I grew
ears made from the same blood as the
women who already knew the deal. that
brown and black women were easy to feel. so we
hid our hips, all to conceal, the sexuality they
told us not to reveal. but they didn't tell us this,
that when they felt us, they felt us with fists.
watched us shrink as they hovered over
our shaking lips. I think I hated myself
even before my first real emotion. almost like I
could see the bodies like mine at the bottom of the
ocean. the women stolen from home and dragged
onto boats. thrown overboard if they became ill en
route, only then learning they can't float.
all because of some bile in their throat. can you see the
ocean bottom? covered in bones like lumps of oats?
I think I hated myself. tried so hard not to look like this.
from doctors' scripts to wax strips. but why was it that
they cursed our hips and laughed at our lips? but when
their own girls had them they called it,
"the face that launched
a thousand ships." why did they hate us like this?

I think I hated myself. but one day I came home to my skin after a lifetime of exile, I met myself at the door like a mother waiting for her child. with tears and a worshipping smile.

come now, baby. I've been waiting on you for a while.

"Bad Muslim" or "A Case for the Ramadan Muslim"

In the 30 days that we
fan the moon as an opulent queen,
the bad Muslim grabs a palm branch.
Shuffles back to the minaret-emblazoned rugs
from which they wandered all of the
other nights of the year.
Nowhere else to stand when all of the devils
are chained.

The bad Muslim is as bad.
As the bad Jew. As the bad Hindu. As the bad Jain.
But the bad Muslim,
now gaping at the roja moon
listening for the woodwind breath of revelation
is somehow more offensive
than any other bads.
For the bad Muslim dares to be
transient, unfixed, open to redemption
unwilling to accept a single dimensional self.
Even if it doesn't stick around much longer
this year.

❧❧

the poetry scares me.
know that I am showing
you my naked body.

❧❧

Wild Thing

in my parents' country
they discovered spiders big enough to
eat small dogs.

the interior jungles are so
dense with vegetation. so wild
that the only equivalent to the
free-roaming wild cats are
the hearts of the people who run
beside them,
and those who have peopled the shore.

you would laugh, you know?
to know that I used to lament
that I did not come from resort beaches.
from umbrella'd drinks and bands performing
in floral button-downs.
you see, I did not yet understand what
it means to be from,
to derive from,
to contain,
such a wilderness. a
homeland that is raw and exists
without the interruptions of
pretty mahals
or havelis.

this wilderness is so selfless,
it will save you and you won't even know it.
carving from itself to give to you.

Chief Kai,
rowing himself over the falls. believing
he could sacrifice himself
to save his people.

who am I to forsake that redemption
for rum and coke on the beach.
for the lure of bejeweled carnivals and
sexy turtle bays.

I come from blazing hot sun.
I come from a shoreline that flirts with the equator,
wind that makes love with the trees at high noon
in a most sweltering
heat that proclaims their passion to the world.
I come from generations of migrants reduced to
oral histories that are
cratered by the fallacy of memory.
I come from brown and black skin
from bones cracking under the weight of
finding work.
Any work at all.

I come from a network of rivers
with names that command the
full
use of
your tongue.

—continued

I come from Potaro and
Rupunini and
Mazaruni.

I come from Demerara.
and the Demerara gave its blood to give
sweetness to the world, and bled into me so that I can
stand
    here
today and say *death to the sugar trade*
because?
I am wild.

Goodbyes, Part One

I am learning to add fractions
when my grandma tells me
that my Grandpa Boston—her brother
that I call Grandpa,
having no grandpa of my own, so she
has started me a collection of them—will
be visiting to say goodbye.

She says he will be here tomorrow,
will be flying in from Texas
to visit all of the family one last time
before his cancer takes him away to that
place she describes as everythingness and nothingness
all at once.

I am already in such a state. Not
knowing what to say for such a final,
such a ceremonious adieu. I begin a
search for strings of words sufficient to be the last,
to echo into the vastness of this grandpa's
forever.

Before I can formulate a linguistic plan,
before I can rehearse my diction and
practice my gestures,
he walks through the frame of Grandma's side door.
His usually round cheeks are sunken like pillaged
half marrow bones
and his skin has the glow of a
premature nimbus.

—continued

He stands with my grandma awhile as she bakes
in the kitchen,
and I turn away, not able to look on at what
private things they might share. I sit down
in the living room with an aunty who has come
to say her last goodbye, too.

When this grandpa finally walks into the living room,
the cartoon network is the backdrop for his solemn duty.
He hugs that aunty, him standing,
her sitting
Her tear-stained face tucked into his still-round belly,
clothed in off-white jersey.

This grandpa conveys to me the usual
directives. *Study hard* and *Be a good child*.
And I merely nod and smile and
hug back when he hugs.

I am surprised by the low burn of this moment.
In my mind I had engineered what such a goodbye should
entail. And I decided that, if it were me,
I would invite everyone to
my home, where there would be a long dinner table
filled with all of my favorite foods.
And maybe live music so
that we can dance together one last time.
And maybe lots of games
so that I can be remembered as fun.
And maybe little envelopes of cash for everyone
to take home
because what else do you do with that stuff when you die?

This grandpa's simple coming and going
seemed like a very underwhelming goodbye to me.

This grandpa leaves
Grandma's house through the same side door
to go off and complete his tour.
Saying his goodbyes throughout the
labyrinths of Queens,
and then the vertical cities of the Bronx.
Leaving each home as a final, immortal
memory as he enters through
doorframes, leaves through doorframes. Forever.

I am angry with myself for not offering any
words of my own. Now what great sounds will my nods and
smiles reverberate in that place of
everythingness and nothingness?

But I have never said goodbye before.

Goodbyes, Part Two

I am in college when, after months of denial,
stove burners left on
and bank PINs lost, Grandma
accepts that her memory is
an hourglass nearing the end of
its grain.
In those very last moments of pouring sand,
she asks me the favor of a ride.
She has a list of places she wants to go
before she cannot remember them anymore.

I enter through the side door and she is almost ready
to leave. Jacket and gloves, a knit hat on her head.
She stuffs money into a few envelopes with greeting cards
and decides she is ready.
There is no holiday approaching, and I wonder what
cards she chose for *this*.
Goodbye? Good luck? Blank?

We drive to her friends' home at the
other end of the A-train.
We drive to my other granny's house.
We drive to see Aunty in Brooklyn.
We drive all through Queens.
She gives each person a card with the cash inside. They are
confused by this gift. But grandma does not tell them why.
When we leave each house,
I know there are puzzled faces left behind.
I feel their gazes on our backs as we walk away.

I imagine the phone calls they make as we drive off.
"Did she visit you today?"

At one house, she forgets that she has already given a
card, and takes out more money to gift. I am confused,
but do not say anything.
When we leave the last house, she asks to go to
her favorite restaurant where she
places an order for one of each of her favorite dishes.
She eats a little bit of each in a carousel fashion.
After four spins she decides she is satisfied.
In the car home, she counts her money as the sky becomes
whipped lavender and realizes
her mistake giving the extra money.
Why didn't you tell me! she chastises.

But I have never said goodbye this way before.
Where there is no journey to
that place of everythingness and nothingness,
but instead a preparation for the halfway departure
of the memories from their flesh. Forever.

Goodbyes, Part Three

I am mothering my first child when I decide what will be
the nature of my own goodbyes.
Should I have the good (good?) fortune of
such preparation.

I will visit everyone I love. And everyone who loves
me.
Entering doorframes. Leaving doorframes.
I will embrace them all long enough
for them to remember my smell because
smell is the memory that stays forever.

And I will thunder into that place
of everythingness and nothingness
with the alacrity of dozens of embraces.

The Immigrant Parent

The immigrant parent only cares about the bottom line.
The immigrant parent doesn't understand why
you must choose
    this uncertain work.
The immigrant parent wants you to be more mainstream.
The immigrant parent doesn't understand inherited trauma.
The immigrant parent doesn't understand how you feel things
    that didn't start with you.
The immigrant parent doesn't see the big deal.
The immigrant parent takes your unhappiness with the status
quo as insults to their sacrifices to bring
you to this status quo.
The immigrant parent believes your dissatisfaction is their
    personal failure.
The immigrant parent is afraid of your right to demand more.
The immigrant parent wants to know why you can't leave well
    enough alone – if you only knew
where we came from.
The immigrant parent is still learning to recognize abuses they
    were taught was love.
The immigrant parent is re-learning how to love.
The immigrant parent is unlearning how they were loved.
The immigrant parent needs patience.
The immigrant parent needs you.
The immigrant parent won't say they need you.
The immigrant parent needs you.

Granny's House, Richmond Hill, Queens

Door

Step out to
waves of stained
asphalt, with zari
borders of
concrete. She
loved to swim.

Living Room

We sit on the bare floor with Styrofoam bowls
of channa and cheese sandwiches.
Our singing almost drowns the slamming of
dominoes.
Of rum cascading into narrow plastic cups.
When the hymns are finished the old people
talk of long time with the departed. Cousins
leave and return with fast food. Garbage bags
later filled with aluminum containers and
sandwich wrappers from the avenue.

Window

an armchair hinges at the side of the glass.
old eyes and gray hair
sit for two generations.
watching diaspora grow
from suckling to
oak.

Stories of back home comfort aching chests, fill the
throats of the grieving, grief is not being familiar
enough with this ghost to mourn.
Granny calls me to help her cold the tea. I create
waterfalls of Red Rose and sugar from enamel cups
until it froths like the Demerara at high tide. Clumps
of Chief Kai falling in the downpour.
I wade and sway through crowds of
people with a tray of teacups.
Grief is diaspora comforted by homes no longer
standing.

Bathroom 1

Kitchen

I hollow slimy grey shrimp of their veins
while my granny grinds fruits,
pours rum, lines pans, answers calls—
scribbles names on the cupboard—
opens and shuts the oven door. Takes
out his food. The Atlantic spills into the
silver basin at my feet, metal and salt.
Her hollowing eyes meet
mine, kindly, as she hands me a coconut
to grate, a slab of metal to sit on.
"Many hands make life work," she says.
"Everything is for you all."

Dining Room

There is nowhere to put down your bag – the room is overcast with black cake,
still more coming.
I do not want to talk about what just happened. But granny must.
I do not want to talk about it. *Why didn't you give me the answers to the*
psychiatrist's questions?
I do not want to talk about it. *I jabbed you in your ribs and you didn't answer me.*
I do not want to talk about it. *Why did you let me say that Bush is the president?*
I do not want to talk about it.
   Why did you let me say 2002, summer, and 'I have no children'?
I do not want to quarrel. Instead, I brace myself for mourning. I begin to mourn,
as I bear witness to her disappearance.
It took this poem for me to learn the day I began mourning.

—inspired by Fatimah Asghar's "Script for Child Services: Floor Plan"

The Side Door

The Study
When he dies and we turn
the key he never let
Granny hold, the air is moldy.
We bow our heads.

Hallway
Leave your shoes
at the door.
Feel hardened frosting
under
your feet.

Maa's Room
Maa dies.
I hide here for months, furious with
my parents.
Granny tucks me in and kisses my
face. Breath smelling of a mouth
dried. Pray with me.
Drink tea with me.
Go to the West Indian store for me.

Maa dies.
I hide here for months.
I try to tuck her in but cakes keep her awake.
Eat your dinner, Gran.
Please come to sleep, Gran.
Can I help you finish early, Gran?

*Call your father, child. Not even God can
love you as much as your parents.*

Bathroom 2
The home aide bathes great
grandma in the tub and
combs her hair
with a fine-teeth comb
ill-suited for her
hair, which is dense like
coconut husk.
It smells like her skin in here.
If I try real hard. I can
still smell her skin sometimes.

Granny's Room
She is old and sleeps two hours per
night.
The doorless closet is spilling
with clothes she never has
reason to wear.
When he leaves she invites
me to nap in the room. But there is
suddenly a smell that reminds me to feel homesick.
This room is so far away from
home. So far away from the rest of this house.

Industry

di way you work
is di way you love,
my gran said to me.
knowing that love is a labor like
any other.

like the codes of life from lands lost,
without knowing it we inherit the way we labor.
we inherit di work
that our bloodline performs; the way we know to love.

my lover. the child.
of cane field workers
wonders why I love him the way I do.
me. the child. of rice planters.

his love so free and flowing,
excitable like sugar straight from cane.
wild like a swift chop to the stem,
a swing of a stack atop the shoulders.

my love so cautious and careful,
executed with precision while combatting
the virtues of reason, ration, restraint.
in the face of messy abandon. apportioning
grains for the stability to survive the
end of a harvest. in sobering fear of the end of harvest.

what a beautiful balance in this dance
of rice and sugar.
of cane and grain.
of work and bellies
always full.

Waiting for a Name

This poem is a rough draft.
Just like my motherland.
It is a draft once crumpled into a ball
only to be reopened and smoothed
and crumpled again.
And now it lays open
bumpy and rough around the edges.
Hard to read through the
lacerations of rejection.

My granny comes from a place
called Wakenaam. She tells me that
it is Dutch for "waiting for a name".
A place someone left half done.
Still waiting to be titled.
But meeting no further iterations.

So many authors have tried to write a story
for this land.
And then laid down their ink by the seawall to full
catfish belly.
But my granny tells me you do not have to be
complete to be whole.
That beauty is as beautiful by any other
name. Or no name at all.

Laundry Day

A single strand of
twine threads two
labyrinths of brick.
Bearing fruits of madras
cloth, socks, working pants.
Hanging stiffly, uncomfortable
in the unwelcome embrace of
January's breath.
The twine ends at a window
encased in metal with hinges
at its hip
nodding toward a microcosm of
three to a bed
ten people fed
at dinner.

A pot marred with soot boils with spices
that somehow made it past customs,
eager to tell stories of home,
its aromatic gossip kissing this new home
on the cheek the way sisters do. Lovingly.
Critically.
Unconditionally.
Ten people fed at dinner
the mother smiles at the fortune of
children who love each other.

Profit and Loss

my grandmother.
a vision in blur
always in motion, a vehicle
for "we must always have money," for
"you must never need his money."

a bus to the end of Queens for job number one.
up until dawn baking black cake for job number two.
in her constant motion the smell of the cakes
from her oven was the only thing that sat with
me as I watched cartoons and
as I did my homework. a constant broken
briefly each day for an embrace in
prayer,
by the extension of her hand holding a
rose-trimmed plate crowned with
food she didn't have time to make.
laying herself in the sun to husk
like the halved limes that lined the
sidewalk after the neighbor's puja.
she felt safe with the steady stream
of customers, of money stowed in six
different purses. immobile and withered
from years of drying sun. ice melted in
heat. I watch my mother sort through
my grandmother's impeccable accounts.
a thorned nest.
a false home.

For Them

—inspired by Olivia Gatwood's "Ode to the Women on Long Island"

I want to write a poem for the people of richmond hill.
who don't able read this poem anyway.

for the people who drag themselves awake to
cross their busts,
or ring puja bells,
or pray namaz.
and for the people who sleep for a few extra minutes
because god nah do nothing fi dem anyway.

for the people who suck their teeth when the conductor
announces a sick passenger on the train because
you know what? they and all don't feel well but they're still
going to work. so why the delay?

I want to write a poem for the people of richmond hill.
who do like they can't hear or see the fifteen men
all at once asking if they need a taxi at lefferts.

for the grannies who stay home to clean house while the kids
work and the grands go to school. who bunjay
their meats in unison
so that as the working people walk home, the scents of curry
make their stomachs cuss their feet for not
moving fast enough.

—continued

for the people on visa
who are looking for any small work at all if you hear anything.
they can build house and mind baby and cook any kind of food
if they watch you do it once.

I want to write a poem for the people of richmond hill.
who leave work early when their kids cut school.
for the people who show up to the hookie jams and tell the DJ
"call he name on the mic so all he friend dem know
I come for he."
for the DJs who comply and laugh till they weep.
for the people who struggle to hide the traces
of their accents even when they try their hardest, so they
implore their children to speak properly
but still forgot to teach them that its plan-tain and not plan-tin.
for the kids who learned the queen's english but still speak
like their parents anyway because
what is home but a bed on the tongue.

I want to write a poem for the people of richmond hill.
for the women who can't believe,
loudly on a public sidewalk,
that sheena dem could treat their sister-in-law suh bad
and are so positive that asif ah do drugs because they catch he
smoking cigarettes—so sad, big meijee son like he.

for the women who stayed with husbands that beat them
just so their children would never know a broken home
or a stepmother who hates them.
for those same women who don't realize
their home is broken, anyway.

I want to write a poem for the people of richmond hill.
who say poetry is not real work.
who are so consumed by
their rent
and their mortgage
and their bills that
they forgot what art feels like and
what a life of inspired labor feels like.

for the people who make sure every house
on the street can hear their new CD
and who always have a plate of food for visitors
no matter how money is tight.
for the people who don't understand this new soca
but still pelt waist with fluency.
who will talk to you late into the night, their eyes heavy
with sleep but will still say, *"wait! where are you going? stay!
there's still some night left."*

for the people who demand your focus when they
instruct you to *"take your education because they
can never take it away from you."*

I want to write a poem for the people of richmond hill.
for the kids who move away and for the parents who
proudly beam about their escape.
"me son got a big house ah long island now," they say.

for the kids who wanted more than anything to get away
but find themselves struggling to recreate the comforts
of home.

—continued

I want to write a poem for the people of richmond hill.
who you can come home to at the end of the worst days.
for the parents and aunts and uncles who will tell their friends
about how you're smart enough to be a doctor.
but will privately tell you all the reasons you are a jackass.

for the people who remind you where you came from when
you feel afraid or inferior. who remind you that you come from
cutting cane at dawn and dabbing bottom house till dusk.
who say that you should never even let the boss talk
down to you
because we've had just about enough of being inferior
to anyone.
for the people who say stand tall and work twice
as hard and,
if they still don't appreciate you,
baby, leave when they need you the most.
small axe does cut down big tree.

I want to write a poem for the people of richmond hill.
who think of the old country and cuss, *"me nah go back deh!"*
and when you say the same and scrunch your nose,
they shout.

"chile, don't ever take your eye and pass wha mek you."

One Last Bag

I've placed these dials back in place so many times,
sometimes with tamarind paste. Queens cousin
done had five stereos
just like this one.
He buys them new every time it break.
Same way, I have the same man,
never mind how many times I was ready to
call for junk.
But Queens cousin done change up he girl three time.
Nothing these people does keep.
How them go keep we?

Three parcels of ginep pillow the stereo
in this one last bag.
Queens cousin said the ginep selling by he too too sour.
Four five jamun fit in each
cassette holder. Queens aunty want
just a taste from her tree.
Never mind she don't come home to mind it.

One coffee jar of achar is pushing it. But I squeeze it between
the crinkly ginep.
I would want someone to make space for me, too,
if I need it.
If any officer go through this bag,
they will get dead to pack this back.
I tie a silky blue ribbon to the luggage handle like a
school girl's braid.
I can lose all but I can't lose this bag. Not this one at all.

Posturing

I scroll through all assortments of living arrangements.
Convinced that I must find somewhere bigger.
Updated and bright.
With a pot filler and modern accent walls.

"I don't want anyone to take their eye and pass her," I justify.

Wanting my daughter to grow up in a home that is grand
    and demands respect.
That is manicured and neat
and will tell her friends that she is
important and valuable.
With bricks neatly stacked to say she is impenetrable.
That she lives in a home that is peopled
with protectors.
Do not try it,
with her.

But here I am, a child of Queens,
having only known
one square of concrete backyard
and bedrooms shared.

And who would ever take their eye and pass me?

Wading

I collect crumbs of my
rightful language the way
people collect stamps and coins and figurines
of characters they wish they could be.
in the most unexpected places we run into each other.
a phrase here, a string of words there.
I practice shoving them across my foreign but
still familiar tongue for days, building
a mismatched vocabulary that I have mourned
since I was my grandmother.

   araam se.
theek hai.
   main dekh nahin sakte?

trying on new clothing in my mouth I play
with words like coveted dolls.
living so many different lives in my mind as I
perfect their intonations.
I talk to the sister who does my eyebrows,
practicing what I know with her,
until I reach the point of high water,
fluids filling my throat
my lungs. and I must swim back
to English. waiting to collect more words
so that I can swim further next time.

Estranged

I wonder how many times
I have gone out into the world.
walked endless streets and gazed
upon countless faces.
and heard my true, rightful mother
tongue but did not even recognize
Her.

Caste: *Musalaman*

From Musalaman: that place where perfumed
begums ruminated in Peshawar courtyards.
Their teeth crystallized with paan
and petals of fleshy poetry fanning their gums.
That place now under a sky of angry, tangled vines of
wire. The azaan the only thing that remembers me.

From Fullaman: that place where Bhojpuri wafted
over cane fields to fall into tahajjud.
Where the namesake is meant to mar and
Urdu is held like a child who fears losing
their mother
in this strange place.

From Muslim: that place where we've managed
to lose mother anyway.
But where we have come to know her best.

All of these places
are mine.

Is

Diaspora is husked ginep on sizzling tar roads.
Diaspora is bathing in blue.
Diaspora is clapping when the plane lands.
Diaspora is a floor freshly wiped with purple cleaner.
Diaspora is dollar store doilies.
Diaspora is you must have three kids, dah way if two fight,
                              the third can bring them back together.
Diaspora is what sweet in goat mouth does be sour
in he backside.
Diaspora is knowing the home name and the 'right name'
for your foods.

> Bora = Chinese string beans.
> Hassa = Armored Catfish.
> Kareila = Bitter Gourd.

Diaspora is what a pound for this?
Diaspora is a Lefferts-bound train.
Diaspora is air horns on chutney.
Diaspora is overzealous DJs on soca.
Diaspora is when yuh guh marrid?
Diaspora is bay rum cologne and cigarettes.
Diaspora is Avon face cream.
Diaspora is how Princess Diana been nice.
Diaspora is Jim Reeves on loop.
Diaspora is noint dah baby so she waist go be small.
Diaspora is silk flowers wearing crystals of plastic dew.
Diaspora is Guyana tun real bad, bai.
Diaspora is ayo can fit this in yuh suitcase for me nah?

Diaspora is when stupidness been ah share you tek all.
Diaspora is arre baap.
Diaspora is dis ting wan mo salt.
Diaspora is after laugh come cry.
Diaspora is share laugh.
Diaspora is share cry.

What a Pound

Seeking a mile of skin as
luscious
        as a fleshy wiri wiri.

Thick with seeds.
        Eyes water at the thought of its heat.
To hold between fingers. Mash with a little rice.
        A little lentil for diffusion.

Borrow wind through sucking lips.
Borrow sea in dousing drink.
        It hot but it eat nice.

We have so much in common,
you and I.
Scorching Earth
        to grow again.

Salaam Means They Have Rights Over You

my granny always said
we should greet the moon with
"salaam".

is there any peace in that power that causes the
rising tide to whip the faultless shores?
or in the force that causes the coyote
to holler in haunting agony?

is there any peace in the way it forces
seeds into sprout,
just as your mother hoists your chin during a
scolding?

are we greeting it with peace in acknowledgement,
or are we pleading for it?

A Guide for Nointing Your Baby

fill your palm with oil.
rub your hands together to create warmth.
start with the legs.

massage each leg so that it stretches out straight. bend
them to the stomach.

fill your palm with oil.
assure her that she is more than
this body. that this body
is merely a vessel for the intangible treasures it carries.

> kiss him so he knows it is
> okay for boys to show affection.

massage the arms and bring them overhead.
and then all the way down. criss-cross them
over the chest.

> when men begin to notice her, protect
> her from all of the ways it will feel like weapons
> have been drawn.

> forbid him from weaponry.

fill your palm with oil.
moisten the mole completely. do not
let the scalp sit dry.
trace over the eyebrows with your forefingers and
kiss the meaty

bulb of the nose with your thumb.
                    let them pursue the subjects they love.
                    teach them how to eat
                       no matter the earnings.
fill your palm with oil.
squeeze the bum in your palms. shape it into a heart.
trace your fingers down the spine.

when their hearts are broken
mend with too-sweet tea
and blocks of frozen condensed milk.
tell them there is no one else like them,
anywhere. you've looked.

cross the left leg with the right arm.
cross the right leg with the left arm.
stretch. stretch. stretch.

show them that there is no
conceivable reality where
life without them
would ever be the same.
that there are people
counting on them to come home
each day.
pile their limbs into a neat mountain of flesh
atop their chest. place both hands on this heap
and tap to the count of three. then, clap and release the limbs
so that they spill in all directions.

—continued

they will laugh a gummy laugh.
smile and cheer!
kiss their smiling cheeks.

there will be days their cheeks will taste of salty sadness.
show them
how things bend and twist and fall apart
and, still, come together again.

me been dream fish.
 but nah tell nobody. dem go bad eye yo.
eclipse ah come tomorrow. stay inside, nah
fold or cut.
di baby twist. leh yo aunty turn am round.
dah pain yo? gyal, you nah know pain yet.
okay. now yuh know pain.
eat ah halwa. bubby go get nuff milk.
must noint dah child waist and bamsey.
keep am inside and next week show am sun.
shave ah head.
bury ah navel string ah yard.
        you know whey you wan deh?
tie black bead pon ah wrist.
put black pot pon ah foot.
stay home. me left eye ah
jump. he gums wan lil rum.
feed am mo.

me been dream fish.

write.
and they can
never interrupt
you.

write.
and they can
never misquote
you.

❧❧

write.
and you will
be
immortal.

❧❧

my entire life boils down
to the fruition of a series
of sacrifices made by people who
loved me, some
without knowing me.

I am undeserving of the
boons of their hardships. of this calm
after the violence.
but there is poetry in an existence like this.
                    pained, gorgeous poetry.

After weeks and weeks of no rain and no Blue Barrel Rainwater, Bibi Zaheeda decided to leave her home of persimmon to seek out any house with leftover rainwater, so she could bottle just enough to take back home with her until the rains returned.

And so she tied her head with green cloth to keep the sun from baking her scalp, and she walked and walked and walked, seeking rainwater from dozens of houses the colors of papaya and soursop and pine, only to find the rainwater had long dried up there, too.

That afternoon, while she rested on the roadside after hours of walking, a man resembling the sturdiness of a cane stalk stopped to ask where she was going. In her desperation, Bibi Zaheeda told The Man about the problem of her ugliness and of the Blue Barrel Rainwater and of the skies that refused to rain. And to this The Man responded that he had many Blue Barrels of Rainwater at home to which she could help herself.

Do You Have Any Idea
What You Are Doing?

having a problem with
Blackness
is having a problem with the Creator.
it is rejecting
something bigger
than all of us.

I'm Not the Problem

if my empowerment
disturbs you,
it is not because I am too
aggressive, or too
sensitive,
but because
your perception of superiority
necessitates my obedience
to your voice,
my politeness to your
disrespect.

Lessons on Vinegar

you can catch more flies with
sweet, sticky honey. but I
just don't understand since when
everyone deserved honey.

Reject. All of it.

there is no goodness
in doing good for
the purpose of good
coming back to you.
goodness is not self-serving.
does karma, then, mean that your
pain.
your illness.
your poverty.
your adversity.
is deserved?

Self-assess

please. think.
of the people you have eaten
from. who feed you.
who keep you full.

have you fed them too?

May God Treat Us the Way We Treat Each Other

I am not interested in your
blind advocacy
or sweeping declarations.
show me, instead.
show me how the women's section
of your masjid compares to the men's.
show me a menstruating woman
performing aarti at your altar.
show me, I pray beg, who your
preacher casts blame upon
            for the fall
                    of Adam.
tell me all about your faith in
practice, without telling me a
word.

Food Is Political

look at all of the
history
written on this table.
in the tangy swank
and mounds of rice
and fragrant stews
and spices that I've learned
to measure with hunches and gut
feelings.
you can taste my entire story.
here.
but you only ever learned to devour.

Things 2020 Taught Me to Never Take for Granted:

1. A standing ovation in a crowded theater.

2. Listening to the bootleg CDs for sale while on a packed roti shop line.

3. Your joke landing with a group of friends at dinner.

4. An off-key aunty singing at a wedding house.

5. Giving a different name at Starbucks every morning.

6. A night of dancing, followed by the halal cart.

7. Bumping into an old, familiar face unexpectedly.

8. Tasting iron in my mouth after a long run in the park.

9. The satisfaction of a meal prepared by someone else.

10. A sleepless night due to the endless possibilities of tomorrow.

Perception Is Not Fact

there was a puma they called
     Karime
for the way his coat resembled
the many hours after sunset when
the foliage barred all wind
all moon.
floating green eyes, each night,
in the darkness
mandible foaming with spit
phalanges pushing into the dirt.
each morning Karime's own paws
betrayed
                his movements.
  his ritual of descending
the highest tree
each night
stopping at the tribe's base to stretch
his legs after the journey. just to ascend
to the
highest
branch
once more
before dawn.
and each night the tribe slept in the
same space,
next to the tracks of paws,
as big as the prints of two men.

         knowing that glowing eyes
         do not mean bared
                teeth.

when you tell me that I'm
"so pretty for a brown girl,"
  I am not flattered
  I do not blush. my skin does
  not flush with heat at these
  pebbles that you mistake for jewels.
  instead I say a silent prayer
  as I stare at you with
  blank eyes.
  pleading with your ancestors
  not to exile you from the
  home of your blood
  just yet.

Lessons on Being an Ally

recognizing your
privilege is just the beginning of your feat.
you must then recognize that it is
unfair.
that you do not deserve it.

Ecosystem

what is a friend
but another source of oxygen?
What is a lover
but your lungs themselves?

Volume

That
silence
of yours.
Did you know that it
kills people
too?

you say you don't see color.
as though observing color is
what is wrong.
as though acknowledging our differences is
wrong.
as though you have chosen to pluck out
your eyes to avoid gazing upon the
ways we suffer in ways you don't.

you say you don't see color.
but we are right here.
burning before you.

How Else Do We Eat?

hatred doesn't always look like narrowed brows,
screaming
voices dripping with venom,
or eyes bulging in anger.

sometimes it looks like someone
quietly
gnawing at their own flesh.

Intuition?

My ancestors knew when India no longer
felt like home.
When Bareilly dawns felt like zip ties on ankle bone.

My parents knew when Guyana no longer
felt like home.
When there was no patriotism that could inspire their loyalty to
that scarcity disguised as tropics.

Will my body ever let me know
when a new home is calling?

The Tenderest Places in the World: A List

a man tying another man's tie, because he doesn't know how.

a child saying hello to a stranger in a passing vehicle.

a mentor bidding farewell to their mentee.

airport drop-offs.

the throes of a father's heart that has been trained to be hard.

children running barefoot across the masjid floor.

a friend buying a meal for a friend.

hardened eyes finding beauty in a poem.

the thankful heart of someone who has received a boon they were convinced they did not deserve.

the love of accepting an apology.

the love of apologizing.

cooking with someone else's stomach in mind.

discovering something magical about yourself.

Seeing magic where there is none at all.

Ungrateful

If words be my life's blood
then perhaps that is why they have the
power
to hurt me so much.
Like my own children striking me down.

༈

Overjoyed, Bibi Zaheeda jumped up from the roadside and pulled the green cloth off her head, and allowed the wind to comb her hair like an ite palm in breeze.

And at this moment The Man smiled, his pupils wide as an eclipsed sun, at the sight of this woman who had convinced herself she was ugly.

"Wait," he said before taking her hand in his. "What is so ugly about the woman leaping before me? With hair that jumps for joy, sharing in your happiness? With blemishes that testify to the life living under your skin and a complexion that mimics the very Earth that gives life and swallows the dead?"✳

༈

Linguistics

I know very well the language of
holes in the walls and
tears shattering into a million
pieces of glass.
you know very well the language of
putrid words woven with regret and
suffering bound into neat packages of closed fists.
can we forgive each other for our
mother tongues?

Curriculum

he doesn't know how to love you.
because the people who were tasked
with teaching him
prioritized that he knew how to be a man first.
a version of a man that has no recollection
of ever being housed by a woman.
and with that education
that man cannot love anyone right.
                    not even himself.
clenched fists outnumbering
praying hands,
tears stifled by commands and slaps
                    boys don't cry.
        where do all the tears go that boys don't get
            to cry? do they evaporate into formlessness,
or do they reincarnate as the tears of women who love them?
horned beasts frighten even the creatures upon
which they do not
prey. and she doesn't understand why he cannot love her
the way she craves.

she doesn't understand why he's never saying sweet things or
even got her some small fresh blooms.
        but the smell of flowers reminds him of his father's funeral
                    and the tears he wasn't allowed to cry.
            and he's never seen a man say nice things to his mom.
                    but he always asks her if she's eaten
or if she needs an extra buck for lunch.
that was the only education he ever got.
so many lessons drowned in tears never wept.

Vision

I only wanted to see you
so that you could see me.

I wanted to give you new eyes.
to see all of the light I shine.
in spite of you.
despite you.
notwithstanding.
you.

❦❦

do you know how many times
I wanted nothing but to spill
open before you,
  but farmed a field between us
instead?

❦❦

Masculinity

some of the most
hurtful
words I've ever heard
came from the mouths of men.

they were never the right person at the
wrong time.
if they were right,
then by now you
would have each learned
the taste of timelessness.

how did you know to find me here?
after such a long period of pedantic
disjunction
                    of c a l c u l a t e d separation.
you have the nerve to know
that I would be here, at this moment.
at this time.
I have become so many other people since we last met.
but where I am in this moment is the same.

I hate that you knew.

There Are Labors of Love and Then There Are Labors for Love

you see the way I have to teach you how to love me?
that's how I know you're not the one.
the way you feel when you're around me should be
your only guiding force.
not my cries and anger pleading for you to understand.
so please. let me go.
so I can be with the one whose energy matches mine.
this is too heavy
for me to carry.
please let me put it down.

if I could re-write my name
in a million different ways
to be more like you
wanted me to be.

I would leave it just so.
etched in onyx.
unchanged. unmoved.

for even this grand schism was written for us.

Curriculum, Part Two

some men.
just cannot love you.
because no matter how much love
women have gifted them.
their fathers have left them so
empty.
they have no idea
what a loving man
looks like.

Trust Your Gut

gut feelings
are energies sent
to you as gifts
from loved ones
on other planes.

For All the Things Your Eyes Have Missed

when my father's family greets me,
they are bewildered by how much
I resemble my grandfather.
when my mother's family greets me,
they marvel at the way they see her
face imprinted on my own.
I suppose that, in all that we do,
we search for the things we love
the most. manifesting the beloved
where it may not exist.
straining to pick them up, these
tiny seeds bedded in unfamiliar
fields. and I wonder: have I done
this to you? drinking you in with
my gaze. never seeing all your
parts.

for the women with eyes so filled with love
they are blind to the horrors they dance with.

Separate Your Destinies from Destinations

there are two kinds of life-changing lovers.

the ones who make you ashamed of the
best parts of yourself.
And the ones who make you wonder
since when you contained all this magic.

Atherosclerosis

when the heart is tired
it builds walls around each of its chambers
with bricks so tightly laid that
not even the wind of a visitor's breath
can find welcome.
the heart locks all doors and seals all windows.
just so that it can finally.
rest.
but with walls so high. no one is able to enter.
to wake it from sleep.

A Womxn's Heart

she leaves you mentally
long before you realize,
long before she decides upon
her physical absence.
for we know how to be tender even
in destruction.
especially in destruction.

❧❧

saying that you can only give so much.
is not selfish.
it is not weak.
it is necessary
for your boundaries.
and their expectations.

❧❧

if I cannot be honest with myself
then I have nothing to offer you
but false peace. a house
collapsible by a whisper
that might awaken me from this sleep
that we have grown to love
so much.

❦❦

you do not believe in the spirits.
the spirits do not believe in you.
my memory
is your only haunting.

❦❦

Stunned, Bibi Zaheeda did not even feel the steamy tears as they dripped down her cheeks, never having heard her ordinary features described in this way before. She took The Man's other hand in hers and examined this face, these eyes, that did not think it necessary for her to be doused in the Blue Barrel Rainwater she had so painfully been seeking.

With both of their hands in each other's, The Man guided Bibi Zaheeda to his house the color of guava flesh, where the Blue Barrels of Rainwater sat politely, in a disciplined line, along his yard's perimeter.

❦❦

sometimes I feel it is a privilege to be a
woman. no one
nurtures one another the way
women do.
men are not allowed to
weep in the arms
of their brothers.
my sisters kiss my
tears.

❦❦

The Art of Being a Big Sister

my ceiling.

is her floor.
what could make me happier than that?

Girl Child

"it's a girl!" I beam.
  She embraces me in loud congratulations
  as onlookers smile.
  She squeezes my arms as she pulls away.
  Bringing her mouth, in a whisper as boisterous as
  doily lace, to my ears.

"don't worry, sister. the next one. will be a boy."

  and
        I
              d r o w n

in the most crushing sadness. Not because she sees no
value in the daughter I am carrying.
But because she sees no value in her own.

Nazar

the evil eye lives not in darkness. not
in hiding or in the shadows of
whispered secrets. it parades in
the light. kisses your cheeks.
tells you how great it is to see you
and that you should come
over, some time. it cannot believe
how much you've grown and wishes
you the best in all you set out to do.
the evil eye never weaves with
cruel thread. it feels everything like love.

on some days you will please
everyone around you.
you will say and do all the right things.
your eyes will exude light upon bare strangers.
and on some days you will please
no one.
you will make mistakes and stumble
each step of every hour.
your eyes will liquify in self-loathing. you will
collapse into a curvy black cloud.

both of these people are worthy of love.

꽃꽃

I have been apprehensive.
even resistant. of meeting
the women that I
have been
              before now.
but I will be kinder to the
women in me that I am
yet to meet.
I will greet them, each time,
with a hug. introduce myself.
ask about her desires.
about what serves her
higher purpose.
tell her that she is welcome
to stay
for as long as she needs.

꽃꽃

when was the last time
that you craved something?
so much that your nerves
ignited in desire and
your mind would not focus
until you had it?

I hope that it was long ago
because
you have gotten into the habit of
fulfilling all of
your hungers.

ᘐᕊ

when your sadness comes to visit,
allow it to stay the night.
speak to it and feed it.
wipe its tears.
stir it some sweet tea with cardamom in an enamel mug.
tuck it into bed, next to you.
kiss it goodnight.
and then in the morning, politely ask it to leave.
make it clear that it is not to be your houseguest.
that you will not allow it to skin you alive.
and when it leaves,
wash the sheets.

ᘐᕊ

Self-Care: A Guide, Part I

hold the side button until it sleeps.
off and disconnected. stand beneath
a torrential stream of water. beating
your skin in percussion. punching
the poison out of your pores with tiny
molecular fists. banishing the dirt
interlaced in your tresses. dry yourself with an old, rough
towel. soothe yourself with its
familiar abrasion. coat your skin in
unrefined coconut oil. mash the jelly
between your fingers and spread its
sweat in shiny half-moons. wash
your hands before embracing
your face with lavender oil. adorn your
frame with the softest clothing you can
find. leave your hair to dry in the air,
becoming frizzy as the minutes pass.
crown your plate with tradition. eat
with your hands. BURN INCENSE.
cleanse the space around you.
breathe it in. navigate your energies.
escape into a book, a show, a song.
become so enmeshed in the character, the
plot, the lyrics, that you forget that they
only live within their medium. submit to the
sweet release of sleep.
awaken with skin, soft and healed. hair, puffed
with the bloating happiness of your nature.
a resolve, renewed. the purest form of you.

Self-Care: A Guide, Part II

make a list of the things you crave the most
in life.

        working more, working less.
        loving more, loving less.
        being more, being less.

make a list of the things that make you feel happy, secure.

        certain company? a certain number of dollars?
        mending a relationship?
        ending? a relationship?

make a list of all the things you want to be.

        spiritually. physically. personally.

make a list of the things you are doing in your life right now.

        reconcile your lists.
        this is your plan.

You collapse into the
ground with your labor.
only for the soil to reject the
vibrations of your seedlings.
Shelled-up luminance
cloaked as grunge.
you weep in the lie
of soiled seeds.

Give Me *That* Life

I kicked my mother with my
tiny feet as she slept,
just to have it.
I wanted it so bad that I
came into the world one
month early, shrieking for it.

this morning a
delicate white-tipped dove asked
me what love feels like. I looked at her,
her small
frame balanced on pinkish sticks
spilling into claws, and I say, *"oh,*
but you fly amongst the grandest love
of all time. How can you not know?"
confused,
she sits silently, a good pupil awaiting
instruction.

"love is that time of day when the sun
has not yet set but the moon
has already risen.
it is the sky gifting us a painting of a lover
who could not wait to see their love."

You're Not Busy and That's Okay

I want you to know that the
delicious silence
is just as meaningful as the
sumptuous noise.

and that the
nothingness is just as
necessary as the chaos.

2020, As Told by the Walls of Your Home

Is World War III in we tail.
All ah we go get we dead.
Di whooole ah Australia ah bun.
End of days reach.
Couple more morning and this ting gone.
Is just a flu. You nah go hear nothing more about it.
Dem mek this ting fi kill we out.
Do not leave dis house.
But is yuh own uncle birthday, how yuh nah go?
Dis country wicked, eh?
Dem cops wicked, eh?
I ain able watch no debate.
Dem this ah quarrel like two old fowl cock.
Yuh aunty dem in Canada nah gah work. Dem get paid lock down.
Such is life. I go work and get me dead.
Me nah tek no vaccine.
Must get the Moderna if you have sense in you head.
Fauci get Moderna and he still nah dead.
Dis body dead.
Dah body dead.
How to use this Zoom?
Y'all can hear me? Okay good.
Dah man go win again, watch.
Wuh! Dah man lose!
This country nice, eh?
Watch how he ah carry on.
Dis country wicked, eh?
Nah skin teeth too much for di new year.
Fish ah play ah sea,
he nah know watah ah boil fuh am.

Empowered

when the wedding drums
no longer drummed
like war drums.

that was the first sign that she was free.

Shahadah

my body is a temple.
join me in worship.

Love without Ownership

"and then he told me that I'm
   beautiful," she told him.
   Looking down at his bowl of coconut rice
   he smiled, pushing the meats of his
   cheeks into his eyes.
"you're not upset?" she quizzed.
"no, I am happy," he finally offered.
"I am happy that someone also sees
   what I see."

What Is Love but a Homeland

take a lover who sees you
as their homeland.
speaks to you in the fluent
comfort of a mother tongue.

he would die in many wars
for my face.
for him.
there is no place like
me.

The Only Constant

a bucket full of prunes
and raisins
went to soak in an amniotic sac of rum
the very evening they promised
themselves to each other.
and even when the sparring began
when the invitations were ripped
when the gossip rippled
when tears shed.
the night before the wedding
the cake baked
and it broke itself into a hundred pieces
of sacrifice
wrapped in wax paper and placed in
paper boxes imprinted with names emblazoned with
gold foil.

so that all of the guests can taste how much they are loved.

❦

that

feeling.

when my

muscles

are

tensed

and

teeth are

clenched

and

temples

are

radiating.

and

you   come   along   and

completely   unravel   me.

❦

The Day I Drank the Universe

when I kissed him
I felt these sparks
on my tongue.
I pulled away in
alarm. just to find
his mouth was filled
with stars. just like me—containing
many worlds at a time. with
nebulae clamoring in
crescendo. with magnetism carried
in swarms of light.

It Will Never Be Enough Time

the moment we knew
THIS was right:

    if we could live for
         one hundred more
  years. if God could give us
         one hundred more years on
  Earth. if we could have
         one hundred more years together.

    it would still be devastating.

Moksha

by the time I began loving you
I had already lived
so many lives.

but this incarnation is my favorite.

Destiny

I have learned that
what is meant for you
will not feel like a needle in your heart.

what is meant for you
will not allow you to reject the most magical
parts of yourself.

what is meant for you
will not make you
choose.

what is meant for you
will not make you
guess.

what is meant for you
will not need more time
to consider.

what is meant for you
will never be
toxic.

what is meant for you
will feel like coming home.

what is meant for you
will feel like activating all
of your dormant talents.

what is meant for you
will sometimes feel like fear because
"when will my luck run out?"
what is meant for you
will feel like disbelief and then
like alleluia.

what is meant for you
will be your rebirth.

ᘰᘮ

with me.
it will never be unclear.
goddesses do not mumble or whisper.
picking the limbs of Uqba from my teeth.
cleaning the blood of Mahishasura
from underneath my fingernails.
the mother is an explosion
of clarity.
I am certainty in flesh.

ᘰᘮ

And just then the skies became dark and thunder rumbled like ceremonial drums in the near distance—a groom approaching the bride's home. All about them, droplets of water began to fall.

Bibi Zaheeda and The Man kept their hands in each other's, and Bibi Zaheeda pulled The Man to dance in the middle of the grass next to his house the color of guava flesh. Wet skin on wet skin, they danced and danced as the first rain in months kissed the ground in grandmotherly affection, their hips knocking over one, two, three, and soon all of the Blue Barrels, with Rainwater flooding their feet and soaking into the soil in parched excitement.

The Man watched as Bibi Zaheeda threw her head and hips about in abandon, and stared in awe as she smiled and collapsed in divine joy into a stream of sweet water, then evaporated into a cirrostratus as delicate as flowers in a dancing girl's hair. The Man mourned the disappearance like a widower from that day forward.

And every year thereafter, on the first day of the rainy season, Bibi Zaheeda would return from her heavenly odyssey around the world to rain down on this very place on the west coast of the Big River, to soak The Man's skin in the same unhinged abandon that she could never forget.

About the Author

photo: Sharifa Khan

Elizabeth Jaikaran is a New York–based author and lawyer, with work published across a spectrum of print and digital media. She began writing at the age of eight and, since then, has published fiction, non-fiction, legal commentary, poetry, and comedy. She is the child of Guyanese immigrants, born in Brooklyn, New York, and raised in Queens.

Jaikaran's writing has appeared in the *Huffington Post, Playboy, The Higgs Weldon, Brown Girl Magazine, Drunk Magazine, SILENT Magazine, Literally, Darling Magazine, The Muslim Observer, Bruk Out Media, PREE Lit, Human/Kind Journal*, and *Defunkt Magazine*.

Her first book, *Trauma: A Collection of Short Stories*, was published by Shanti Arts in 2017, and is recognized as a critically acclaimed work. *Waiting for a Name* is her first collection of poetry.

—lizjaikaran.com

CPSIA information can be obtained
at www.ICGtesting.com
Printed in the USA
BVHW052053220223
658991BV00015B/226